Space

SACREDSPACE

3 DECEMBER 2023 TO 13 JANUARY 2024

FROM THE WEBSITE WWW.SACREDSPACE.IE
PRAYER FROM THE IRISH JESUITS

First published in 2023 by Messenger Publications

Copyright © The Irish Jesuits, 2023

The material in this publication is protected by copyright law. Except
as may be permitted by law, no part of the material may be reproduced
(including by storage in a retrieval system) or transmitted in any form or
by any means, adapted, rented or lent without the written permission of
the copyright owners. Applications for permissions should be addressed
to the publisher.

The right of The Irish Jesuits to be identified as the author of the Work
has been asserted by them in accordance with the Copyright and Related
Rights Act, 2000.

ISBN: 9781788126342

Scripture quotations are from New Revised Standard Version Bible,
National Council of the Churches of Christ in the United States of
America. Used by permission. All rights reserved worldwide.
www.nrsvbibles.org

Weekly reflections are taken from books and periodicals published by
Messenger Publications. For more information go to www.messenger.ie

Designed by Messenger Publications Design Department
Typeset in Adobe Caslon Pro & Avant Garde
Printed by Hussar Books

Messenger Publications,
37 Leeson Place,
Dublin D02 E5V0,
Ireland
www.messenger.ie

Sacred
Space

CONTENTS

The Presence of God

Bless all who worship you, almighty God,
from the rising of the sun to its setting;
from your goodness enrich us,
by your love inspire us,
by your Spirit guide us,
by your power protect us,
in your mercy receive us,
now and always.

How to Use This Booklet

During each week of Advent, begin by reading the 'Something to think and pray about each day this week'. Then go through 'the Presence of God', 'Freedom' and 'Consciousness' steps to help you prepare yourself to hear the Word of God speaking to you. In the next step, 'The Word', turn to the Scripture reading for each day of the week. Inspiration points are provided if you need them. Then return to the 'conversation' and 'conclusion' steps. Follow this process every day of Advent.

The Advent retreat at the back of this book follows a similar structure: an invitation to experience stillness, a Scripture passage and reflection points, and suggestions for prayer; you may find it useful to move back and forth between the daily reflections and the retreat.

The First Week of Advent

3–9 December 2023

Something to think and pray about each day this week:

If you were to wish people a happy new year today, they would in all probability find it awkward. Nevertheless, we do start a new Christian year with the season of Advent. The changing seasons remind us of different aspects of being Christian, one of which is the conviction that we may always begin again and start new. Last Sunday we looked back and today we look forward: What are *my* hopes for the coming Christian year? How am I now? How would I like to be, as a believer, this time next year? What steps will I take to make that a reality?

Kieran O'Mahony OSA,
Hearers of the Word: Praying & Exploring the
Readings for Advent & Christmas

The Presence of God

Dear Jesus, I come to you today longing for your presence. I desire to love you as you love me. May nothing ever separate me from you.

Freedom

Lord, grant me the grace to be free from the excesses of this life. Let me not get caught up with the desire for wealth. Keep my heart and mind free to love and serve you.

Consciousness

Where do I sense hope, encouragement and growth in my life? By looking back over the past few months, I may be able to see which activities and occasions have produced rich fruit. If I do notice such areas, I will determine to give those areas both time and space in the future.

The Word

God speaks to each of us individually. I listen attentively, to hear what he is saying to me. Read the text a few times, then listen. *(Please turn to the Scripture on the following pages. Inspiration points are there, should you need them. When you are ready, return here to continue.)*

Conversation

What is stirring in me as I pray? Am I consoled, troubled, left cold? I imagine Jesus standing or sitting at my side, and I share my feelings with him.

Conclusion

Glory be to the Father, and to the Son, and to the Holy Spirit,
As it was in the beginning, is now and ever shall be,
World without end. Amen.

Sunday 3 December
First Sunday of Advent
Mark 13:33–37

Jesus said to his disciples, 'Beware, keep alert; for you do not know when the time will come. It is like a man going on a journey, when he leaves home and puts his slaves in charge, each with his work, and commands the doorkeeper to be on the watch. Therefore, keep awake – for you do not know when the master of the house will come, in the evening, or at midnight, or at cockcrow, or at dawn, or else he may find you asleep when he comes suddenly. And what I say to you I say to all: Keep awake.'

- The Advent season recalls significant events and people to help us to be alert for Christmas. Qualities such as being prepared and staying attentive are highlighted today. May we grow in appreciation of God's greatest gift to us in Jesus and be ready to welcome him on his coming anew to us.

- Good servants await the return of the master. Our master desires to serve us. May our Advent waiting be one that desires to welcome a friend who comes to save, not a thief in the night who is to be feared.

Monday 4 December
Matthew 8:5–11

When he entered Capernaum, a centurion came to him, appealing to him and saying, 'Lord, my servant is lying at home paralysed, in terrible distress.' And he said to him, 'I will come and cure him.' The centurion answered, 'Lord, I am not worthy to have you come under my roof; but only speak the word, and my servant will be healed. For I also am a man under authority, with soldiers under me; and I say to one, "Go", and he goes, and to another, "Come", and he comes, and to my slave, "Do this", and the slave does it.' When Jesus heard him, he was amazed and said to those who followed him, 'Truly I tell you, in no one in Israel have I found such faith. I tell you, many will come from east and west and will eat with Abraham and Isaac and Jacob in the kingdom of heaven.'

- A centurion, an outsider, pleaded with Jesus for his servant who was paralysed and in great distress. In our distress and paralysis we ask for the faith to reach out to you, Lord, and ask you to give us the healing we need.
- The spoken word can be very influential for good or for ill. For the centurion it was sufficient for Jesus to utter it. Lord, your word is one of salvation. May we hear it, respond to it and bring words of comfort to others in turn.

Tuesday 5 December
Luke 10:21–24

At that same hour Jesus rejoiced in the Holy Spirit and said, 'I thank you, Father, Lord of heaven and earth, because you have hidden these things from the wise and the intelligent and have revealed them to infants; yes, Father, for such was your gracious will. All things have been handed over to me by my Father; and no one knows who the Son is except the Father, or who the Father is except the Son and anyone to whom the Son chooses to reveal him.'

Then turning to the disciples, Jesus said to them privately, 'Blessed are the eyes that see what you see! For I tell you that many prophets and kings desired to see what you see, but did not see it, and to hear what you hear, but did not hear it.'

- Jesus who comes is the source of Joy who reveals the Father to us. Intellectuals can fail to grasp the depth of Jesus' message. We are drawn into Jesus' relationship with the Father. May we have childlike faith and trust to accept what Jesus reveals to us, his children.
- Jesus is grateful to the Father for all that was given to him. We are blessed in what we see and hear through what Jesus reveals to us. We pray to rejoice in the Spirit and be prophetic in bringing it to others in Jesus' name.

Wednesday 6 December
Matthew 15:29–37

After Jesus had left that place, he passed along the Sea of Galilee, and he went up the mountain, where he sat down. Great crowds came to him, bringing with them the lame, the maimed, the blind, the mute, and many others. They put them at his feet, and he cured them, so that the crowd was amazed when they saw the mute speaking, the maimed whole, the lame walking, and the blind seeing. And they praised the God of Israel.

Then Jesus called his disciples to him and said, 'I have compassion for the crowd, because they have been with me now for three days and have nothing to eat; and I do not want to send them away hungry, for they might faint on the way.' The disciples said to him, 'Where are we to get enough bread in the desert to feed so great a crowd?' Jesus asked them, 'How many loaves have you?' They said, 'Seven, and a few small fish.' Then ordering the crowd to sit down on the ground, he took the seven loaves and the fish; and after giving thanks he broke them and gave them to the disciples, and the disciples gave them to the crowds. And all of them ate and were filled; and they took up the broken pieces left over, seven baskets full.

- Jesus went up the mountain, but the crowds followed. He cured those in need of healing to the amazement of all. Mountains were places to meet God. Lord, give us a sense of wonder in our meeting with you and heal the scars of life that we carry.

• Jesus had compassion for the people. This was seen in his healing and his provision of food for them. They were hungry for his word and were also physically hungry, having spent three days with him. Lord, may our hunger, inner and outer, lead us to you to satisfy it.

Thursday 7 December
Matthew 7:21.24–27
Jesus said to them, 'Not everyone who says to me, "Lord, Lord", will enter the kingdom of heaven, but only one who does the will of my Father in heaven.

'Everyone then who hears these words of mine and acts on them will be like a wise man who built his house on rock. The rain fell, the floods came, and the winds blew and beat on that house, but it did not fall, because it had been founded on rock. And everyone who hears these words of mine and does not act on them will be like a foolish man who built his house on sand. The rain fell, and the floods came, and the winds blew and beat against that house, and it fell – and great was its fall!'

• The words of Jesus proclaiming the kingdom of God are meant to find a home in the human heart. Calling Jesus 'Lord' needs to be a reality, a lived experience, doing the will of the Father. May we accept you as Lord and live your message in proclaiming your kingdom.

- God's word was lived out by Jesus. We are to build on that solid foundation where our words lead to action. We pray to be houses built on rock that can withstand the storms of life.

Friday 8 December
The Immaculate Conception of the Blessed Virgin Mary
Luke 1:26–38

In the sixth month the angel Gabriel was sent by God to a town in Galilee called Nazareth, to a virgin engaged to a man whose name was Joseph, of the house of David. The virgin's name was Mary. And he came to her and said, 'Greetings, favoured one! The Lord is with you.' But she was much perplexed by his words and pondered what sort of greeting this might be. The angel said to her, 'Do not be afraid, Mary, for you have found favour with God. And now, you will conceive in your womb and bear a son, and you will name him Jesus. He will be great, and will be called the Son of the Most High, and the Lord God will give to him the throne of his ancestor David. He will reign over the house of Jacob for ever, and of his kingdom there will be no end.' Mary said to the angel, 'How can this be, since I am a virgin?' The angel said to her, 'The Holy Spirit will come upon you, and the power of the Most High will overshadow you; therefore the child to be born will be holy; he will be called Son of God. And now, your relative Elizabeth in her old age has also conceived a son; and this is the sixth month for her who was said to be barren. For nothing will be impossible with God.' Then Mary said, 'Here am I, the servant of the Lord; let it be with me according to your word.' Then the angel departed from her.

- Today's feast looks to a new era in God's salvation story. It recalls Mary being prepared for her role as the mother of Jesus, though the reading refers to the conception of Jesus in her womb. Jesus would be born of the family of David, fulfilling God's plan and offering hope for the future. As promised children we pray to continue God's saving story as family members.

- There is the contrast of the greatness of the event of an angel with a surprising message and that of a humble virgin in an obscure village in Galilee. May we have the faith to receive the message of God in the humble settings of our own lives and bring Jesus to birth anew.

Saturday 9 December
Matthew 9:35–10:1.5a.6–8

Then Jesus went about all the cities and villages, teaching in their synagogues, and proclaiming the good news of the kingdom, and curing every disease and every sickness. When he saw the crowds, he had compassion for them, because they were harassed and helpless, like sheep without a shepherd. Then he said to his disciples, 'The harvest is plentiful, but the labourers are few; therefore ask the Lord of the harvest to send out labourers into his harvest.'

Then Jesus summoned his twelve disciples and gave them authority over unclean spirits, to cast them out, and to cure every disease and every sickness.

These twelve Jesus sent out with the following instructions: 'Go nowhere among the Gentiles, and enter no town of the Samaritans, but go rather to the lost sheep of the house of Israel. As you go, proclaim the good news, "The kingdom of heaven has come near." Cure the sick, raise the dead, cleanse the lepers, cast out demons. You received without payment; give without payment.'

- Jesus was the traveller bringing good news of the kingdom and healing. He had compassion for the people as they were 'like sheep without a shepherd'. To facilitate this he desired helpers to gather the harvest. May we have his love and care in reaching out to others, particularly those in most need.

- Jesus took decisive action in spreading the mission in calling the twelve disciples by name and entrusting the same work to them. We are the unlikely ones called at this time and sent out, so we pray for the honesty to respond to his invitation and remain loyal to Jesus.

The Second Week of Advent

10–16 December 2023

Something to think and pray about each day this week:

Advent is the annual season of waiting. We wait for the same reason every year, and we are certain that the One we await – a Person, Jesus, Son of God – will arrive on time. Yet, we find that the waiting is new each year, as Jesus is ever new. Maybe we don't like the waiting, or maybe we enter enthusiastically into Advent, which in some countries now starts in October. Maybe we are happy to wait in patience and quiet.

We wait also to notice where and how God is in our lives. This waiting is often compared to the watchman who waits, noticing all that is happening around him. He's on a height to see the world around him. Advent can be our hill or mountain. Each day we gather something new about God, ourselves and the world.

The way we wait affects how we celebrate and enjoy Christmas. The way we wait may grow in us a new realisation that everything about God, and especially God's Son, is worth our waiting. We wait for the Lord because his day is near. Thanks be to God!

Donal Neary SJ, *The Messenger Advent Booklet:*
Reflections on the Daily Readings

The Presence of God

Dear Jesus, as I call on you today, I realise that often I come asking for favours. Today I'd like just to be in your presence. Draw my heart in response to your love.

Freedom

God my creator, you gave me life and the gift of freedom. Through your love I exist in this world. May I never take the gift of life for granted. May I always respect others' right to life.

Consciousness

Dear Lord, help me to remember that you gave me life. Teach me to slow down, to be still and enjoy the pleasures created for me. To be aware of the beauty that surrounds me: the marvel of mountains, the calmness of lakes, the fragility of a flower petal. I need to remember that all these things come from you.

The Word

The word of God comes down to us through the Scriptures. May the Holy Spirit enlighten my mind and my heart to respond to the Gospel teachings. *(Please turn to the Scripture on the following pages. Inspiration points are there, should you need them. When you are ready, return here to continue.)*

Conversation

What feelings are rising in me as I pray and reflect on God's word? I imagine Jesus himself sitting or standing near me, and I open my heart to him.

Conclusion

I thank God for these moments we have spent together and for any insights I have been given concerning the text.

Sunday 10 December

Second Sunday of Advent
Mark 1:1–8

The beginning of the good news of Jesus Christ, the Son of God.

As it is written in the prophet Isaiah,
'See, I am sending my messenger ahead of you,
   who will prepare your way;
the voice of one crying out in the wilderness:
   "Prepare the way of the Lord,
   make his paths straight"',

John the baptiser appeared in the wilderness, proclaiming a baptism of repentance for the forgiveness of sins. And people from the whole Judean countryside and all the people of Jerusalem were going out to him, and were baptised by him in the river Jordan, confessing their sins. Now John was clothed with camel's hair, with a leather belt around his waist, and he ate locusts and wild honey. He proclaimed, 'The one who is more powerful than I is coming after me; I am not worthy to stoop down and untie the thong of his sandals. I have baptised you with water; but he will baptise you with the Holy Spirit.'

- The Gospel is the good news of Jesus, the Son of God. It moves quickly to John the Baptist, who fulfilled the prophecy of Isaiah in introducing Jesus. He proclaimed repentance in the wilderness, drawing crowds. Lord, may we find you in the wilderness of this time and draw inspiration from John in living simply and announcing your presence.

- A good facilitator does not say too much or draw attention to self. John gives a very good example. May we introduce the Lord, show the way and politely step aside when not needed.

Monday 11 December
Luke 5:17–26

One day, while he was teaching, Pharisees and teachers of the law were sitting nearby (they had come from every village of Galilee and Judea and from Jerusalem); and the power of the Lord was with him to heal. Just then some men came, carrying a paralysed man on a bed. They were trying to bring him in and lay him before Jesus; but finding no way to bring him in because of the crowd, they went up on the roof and let him down with his bed through the tiles into the middle of the crowd in front of Jesus. When he saw their faith, he said, 'Friend, your sins are forgiven you.' Then the scribes and the Pharisees began to question, 'Who is this who is speaking blasphemies? Who can forgive sins but God alone?' When Jesus perceived their questionings, he answered them, 'Why do you raise such questions in your hearts? Which is easier, to say, "Your sins are forgiven you", or to say, "Stand up and walk"? But so that you may know that the Son of Man has authority on earth to forgive sins' – he said to the one who was paralysed – 'I say to you, stand up and take your bed and go to your home.' Immediately he stood up before them, took what he had been lying on, and went to his home, glorifying God. Amazement seized all of them, and they glorified God and were filled with awe, saying, 'We have seen strange things today.'

• The scribes and Pharisees were sitting near to Jesus but were far away from him in their thinking. Others wanted to come near in faith and found a creative way to do so. As your coming draws near, may we have the freedom to bring the paralysed parts of our lives to you for healing.

• This is a story of inner and outer healing, with Jesus indicating priority in his action. As friends of the Lord may we come to him, accepting the help of others in doing so, to receive what he offers

Tuesday 12 December
Matthew 18:12–14

Jesus asked, 'What do you think? If a shepherd has a hundred sheep, and one of them has gone astray, does he not leave the ninety-nine on the mountains and go in search of the one that went astray? And if he finds it, truly I tell you, he rejoices over it more than over the ninety-nine that never went astray. It is not the will of your Father in heaven that one of these little ones should be lost.'

- Seeking one and leaving ninety-nine could seem foolish or greedy. Our God has a different approach, being compassionate in leaving, searching, finding and rejoicing. We pray that we may recognise ourselves as lost sheep and allow the Lord find us.

- The shepherd rejoiced in finding the lost sheep. He did not scold it for wandering away. May we appreciate the Lord's joy in finding us and bringing us back from our wandering ways.

Wednesday 13 December
Matthew 11:28–30

At that time Jesus said, 'Come to me, all you that are weary and are carrying heavy burdens, and I will give you rest. Take my yoke upon you, and learn from me; for I am gentle and humble in heart, and you will find rest for your souls. For my yoke is easy, and my burden is light.'

- Come to me, come back, come follow me, come and see, are familiar phrases to us. We are invited into a deeper relationship by our God of welcome, who desires us to live more fully. Lord, open our hearts to hear your message to come to you, to accept your invitation and respond to it, knowing that you want what is best for us.

- Life has its challenges and difficulties, but the Lord offers rest. We are reminded that the Lord is gentle and humble in heart but does not remove all burdens. Let us turn to the Lord for his help in lightening our burdens that we may walk in in greater peace.

Thursday 14 December
Matthew 11:11–15

As they went away, Jesus began to speak to the crowds about John: 'Truly I tell you, among those born of women no one has arisen greater than John the Baptist; yet the least in the kingdom of heaven is greater than he. From the days of John the Baptist until now the kingdom of heaven has suffered violence, and the violent take it by force. For all the prophets and the law prophesied until John came; and if you are willing to accept it, he is Elijah who is to come. Let anyone with ears listen!'

- John the Baptist was a 'child of promise', born of elderly parents and given a distinctive role in preparing the way for Jesus. The prophecies pointed to him. As children of the kingdom of God may we value our privileged position of sharing all that Jesus has given.
- John proclaimed, 'Repent, for the kingdom of heaven has come near.' Jesus brought about a new kingdom. May we learn to live simply as children of Jesus' kingdom, being guided by the example of John amid the violence and trouble of this time.

Friday 15 December
Matthew 11:16–19

Jesus said, 'But to what will I compare this generation? It is like children sitting in the market-places and calling to one another,

"We played the flute for you, and you did not
dance;
we wailed, and you did not mourn."

For John came neither eating nor drinking, and they say, "He has a demon"; the Son of Man came eating and drinking, and they say, "Look, a glutton and a drunkard, a friend of tax-collectors and sinners!" Yet wisdom is vindicated by her deeds.'

- John the Baptist and Jesus began their mission in a somewhat similar way in calling for repentance. John was an ascetic figure, living in the wilderness and eating what it produced. Jesus went to several parties and associated with tax collectors and sinners. Both took the situation into account in their ministry. In the market-place of this age, we pray that may we have a clear message that is adapted to the situations we encounter, but that holds on to the truth.
- Fasting or feasting can be genuine responses, depending on the situation. Comparing the externals does not do justice to the deeper reality. May we have the wisdom to understand better what is appropriate to each situation and be guided by the inner truth.

Saturday 16 December
Matthew 17:9a.10–13

As they were coming down the mountain, Jesus ordered them, 'Tell no one about the vision until after the Son of Man has been raised from the dead.' And the disciples asked him, 'Why, then, do the scribes say that Elijah must come first?' He replied, 'Elijah is indeed coming and will restore all things; but I tell you that Elijah has already come, and they did not recognise him, but they did to him whatever they pleased. So also the Son of Man is about to suffer at their hands.' Then the disciples understood that he was speaking to them about John the Baptist.

- Elijah was the fiery prophet who proclaimed God's message in very challenging situations. He 'ascended in a whirlwind into heaven' (2 Kings 2:11), and it was believed that he would return before the Messiah was born. John the Baptist was described in similar terms. May we be the new Elijah and be like John with our prophetic voices.

- The prophets had an important place in proclaiming the truth and calling people back from their errant ways. Many, including John the Baptist, suffered for doing so. Jesus saw that the same fate was in store for him. Lord, may we live for you and announce your message, even though it may involve misunderstanding and suffering.

The Third Week of Advent

17–23 December 2023

Something to think and pray about each day this week:

Who do you see when you look at Mary – Our Lady? An aunt of mine was once showing a man around her home and in nearly every room she had some picture or other, depicting (as she likes to call her) 'The Blessed Mother'. The man, possibly not overly religious, was a little perturbed and felt he had to comment: 'You have a lot of pictures of Mary,' he said. Without a flinch my aunt replied, 'Oh, but of course, I consider her a personal friend.' No more to be said!

It's a great way to look at Mary – as a 'personal friend' – and in that light you can see why God would dispatch Gabriel to meet her in the kitchen. He knew what sort she was. There was a generosity of spirit there and a kindness that is only truly found in the best of friends. I think that's how she would want us to see her today as we journey with her to Bethlehem in the company of Joseph. She would want us to see her as someone whose door is open to us – no need for formalities or elaborate ritual. The door is open, the light is on and she awaits our approach.

Vincent Sherlock, *Let Advent be Advent*

The Presence of God

'Be still, and know that I am God.' Lord, your words lead us to the calmness and greatness of your presence.

Freedom

I am free. When I look at these words in writing, they seem to create in me a feeling of awe. Yes, a wonderful feeling of freedom. Thank you, God.

Consciousness

At this moment, Lord, I turn my thoughts to you.
I will leave aside my chores and preoccupations.
I will take rest and refreshment in your presence, Lord.

The Word

The word of God comes down to us through the Scriptures. May the Holy Spirit enlighten my mind and my heart to respond to the Gospel teachings. *(Please turn to the Scripture on the following pages. Inspiration points are there, should you need them. When you are ready, return here to continue.)*

Conversation

Begin to talk with Jesus about the Scripture you have just read. What part of it strikes a chord in you? Perhaps the words of a friend – or some story you have heard recently – will slowly rise to the surface of your consciousness. If so, does the story throw light on what the Scripture passage may be trying to say to you?

Conclusion
Glory be to the Father, and to the Son, and to the Holy Spirit,
As it was in the beginning, is now and ever shall be,
World without end. Amen.

Sunday 17 December
Third Sunday of Advent
John 1:6–8.19–28

There was a man sent from God, whose name was John. He came as a witness to testify to the light, so that all might believe through him. He himself was not the light, but he came to testify to the light.

This is the testimony given by John when the Jews sent priests and Levites from Jerusalem to ask him, 'Who are you?' He confessed and did not deny it, but confessed, 'I am not the Messiah.' And they asked him, 'What then? Are you Elijah?' He said, 'I am not.' 'Are you the prophet?' He answered, 'No.' Then they said to him, 'Who are you? Let us have an answer for those who sent us. What do you say about yourself?' He said,

'I am the voice of one crying out in the
    wilderness,
"Make straight the way of the Lord", '
as the prophet Isaiah said.

Now they had been sent from the Pharisees. They asked him, 'Why then are you baptising if you are neither the Messiah, nor Elijah, nor the prophet?' John answered them, 'I baptise with water. Among you stands one whom you do not know, the one who is coming after me; I am not worthy to untie the thong of his sandal.' This took place in Bethany across the Jordan where John was baptising.

- John the Baptist was a witness and pointed the way to Jesus, the true light. He was clear on his identity and his role, saying he was not the Messiah, or the prophet, but one whose baptism was preparatory. Let us be voices in the wilderness that announce the presence of Jesus, the eternal Word, even if we feel no one is listening.

- John was an object of curiosity, with priests being sent from Jerusalem into the wilderness to investigate. He humbly acknowledged his own role but directed them towards Jesus. In recognising that 'among you stands one you do not know', we may announce Jesus' presence and message in word and in deed.

Monday 18 December
Matthew 1:18–25
Now the birth of Jesus the Messiah took place in this way. When his mother Mary had been engaged to Joseph, but before they lived together, she was found to be with child from the Holy Spirit. Her husband Joseph, being a righteous man and unwilling to expose her to public disgrace, planned to dismiss her quietly. But just when he had resolved to do this, an angel of the Lord appeared to him in a dream and said, 'Joseph, son of David, do not be afraid to take Mary as your wife, for the child conceived in her is from the Holy Spirit. She will bear a son, and you are to name him Jesus, for he will save his people from

their sins.' All this took place to fulfil what had been spoken by the Lord through the prophet:

'Look, the virgin shall conceive and bear a son,
    and they shall name him Emmanuel',

which means, 'God is with us.' When Joseph awoke from sleep, he did as the angel of the Lord commanded him; he took her as his wife, but had no marital relations with her until she had borne a son; and he named him Jesus.

- Mary and Joseph were recipients of the mysterious ways of God. Mary was found to be with child from the Holy Spirit and Joseph wondered what to do. He was given direction in a dream, reminding us of Joseph the dreamer in Genesis. Mary would give birth to a son who would be called Jesus, who would save his people from their sins. Lord, as we prepare for your birth, may we inspired by the faith and example of Mary and Joseph in welcoming you.

- God reassured many who were facing new situations, such as Moses and Jeremiah, with the words 'I will be with you'. May we rely on the fidelity of God and draw strength from Jesus as Emmanuel, God with us, in the challenges of life.

Tuesday 19 December
Luke 1:5–25

In the days of King Herod of Judea, there was a priest named Zechariah, who belonged to the priestly order of Abijah. His wife was a descendant of Aaron, and her name was Elizabeth. Both of them were righteous before God, living blamelessly according to all the commandments and regulations of the Lord. But they had no children, because Elizabeth was barren, and both were getting on in years.

Once when he was serving as priest before God and his section was on duty, he was chosen by lot, according to the custom of the priesthood, to enter the sanctuary of the Lord and offer incense. Now at the time of the incense-offering, the whole assembly of the people was praying outside. Then there appeared to him an angel of the Lord, standing at the right side of the altar of incense. When Zechariah saw him, he was terrified; and fear overwhelmed him. But the angel said to him, 'Do not be afraid, Zechariah, for your prayer has been heard. Your wife Elizabeth will bear you a son, and you will name him John. You will have joy and gladness, and many will rejoice at his birth, for he will be great in the sight of the Lord. He must never drink wine or strong drink; even before his birth he will be filled with the Holy Spirit. He will turn many of the people of Israel to the Lord their God. With the spirit and power of Elijah he will go before him, to turn the hearts of parents to their children, and the disobedient to the wisdom of the righteous, to make ready a people prepared for the Lord.' Zechariah said to the angel,

'How will I know that this is so? For I am an old man, and my wife is getting on in years.' The angel replied, 'I am Gabriel. I stand in the presence of God, and I have been sent to speak to you and to bring you this good news. But now, because you did not believe my words, which will be fulfilled in their time, you will become mute, unable to speak, until the day these things occur.'

Meanwhile, the people were waiting for Zechariah, and wondered at his delay in the sanctuary. When he did come out, he could not speak to them, and they realised that he had seen a vision in the sanctuary. He kept motioning to them and remained unable to speak. When his time of service was ended, he went to his home.

After those days his wife Elizabeth conceived, and for five months she remained in seclusion. She said, 'This is what the Lord has done for me when he looked favourably on me and took away the disgrace I have endured among my people.'

- This is another annunciation story by the angel Gabriel in the more solemn setting of the temple. Zechariah and Elizabeth, both elderly, are promised a child who will be named John and will have the particular mission of bringing people back to the Lord. We pray for openness to the surprising ways of God and recognise that we too have been named for mission.

• The revelation raised questions and doubts of a practical nature for Zechariah, given his age and that of Elizabeth. This is another instance of what God could do. John was going to be the voice but Zechariah lost his voice. Lord, may we turn to you with our doubts so that our tongues do not become mute in revealing God's message.

Wednesday 20 December
Luke 1:26–38

In the sixth month the angel Gabriel was sent by God to a town in Galilee called Nazareth, to a virgin engaged to a man whose name was Joseph, of the house of David. The virgin's name was Mary. And he came to her and said, 'Greetings, favoured one! The Lord is with you.' But she was much perplexed by his words and pondered what sort of greeting this might be. The angel said to her, 'Do not be afraid, Mary, for you have found favour with God. And now, you will conceive in your womb and bear a son, and you will name him Jesus. He will be great, and will be called the Son of the Most High, and the Lord God will give to him the throne of his ancestor David. He will reign over the house of Jacob for ever, and of his kingdom there will be no end.' Mary said to the angel, 'How can this be, since I am a virgin?' The angel said to her, 'The Holy Spirit will come upon you, and the power of the Most High will overshadow you; therefore the child to be born will be holy; he will be called Son of God. And now, your relative Elizabeth in her old age has also conceived a son; and this is the sixth month for her who was said to be barren. For nothing will be impossible with God.' Then Mary said, 'Here am I, the servant of the Lord; let it be with me according to your word.' Then the angel departed from her.

- There was a perplexing message to Mary as favoured by the Lord. Her reaction of wonder, fear and surprise led to a question of how this could be. May we have the openness to hear the message, the freedom to question it and to accept the response, relying on the promise that nothing is impossible to God.

- Perhaps we can note that movement in our own lives – we are asked to do something, which leads us to question why, but then we can be given a sign that leads us to say 'yes'. This may go on over time. We thank you, Lord, for the surprising ways in which you have entered and guided our lives.

Thursday 21 December
Luke 1:39–45
In those days Mary set out and went with haste to a Judean town in the hill country, where she entered the house of Zechariah and greeted Elizabeth. When Elizabeth heard Mary's greeting, the child leapt in

her womb. And Elizabeth was filled with the Holy Spirit and exclaimed with a loud cry, 'Blessed are you among women, and blessed is the fruit of your womb. And why has this happened to me, that the mother of my Lord comes to me? For as soon as I heard the sound of your greeting, the child in my womb leapt for joy. And blessed is she who believed that there would be a fulfilment of what was spoken to her by the Lord.'

- Mary set out on a journey to be with her aged cousin, Elizabeth, in the hill country. It was a meeting of two mothers-to-be, who became pregnant in surprising circumstances. Both could acknowledge God's graciousness to them and be of support to each other. May we have a spirit of gratitude for the new life the Lord has shown us and shared with us.

- This visitation was a meeting of two women of faith who brought joy, comfort and blessing to each other. The presence of their unborn children enhanced the joy of the occasion. May we bring Jesus with us on our visitations, offering hope and promise to those we call to see.

Friday 22 December
Luke 1:46–56

And Mary said,
'My soul magnifies the Lord,

and my spirit rejoices in God my Saviour,
for he has looked with favour on the lowliness
    of his servant.
  Surely, from now on all generations will call
    me blessed;
for the Mighty One has done great things for me,
  and holy is his name.
His mercy is for those who fear him
  from generation to generation.
He has shown strength with his arm;
  he has scattered the proud in the thoughts of
    their hearts.
He has brought down the powerful from their
    thrones,
  and lifted up the lowly;
he has filled the hungry with good things,
  and sent the rich away empty.
He has helped his servant Israel,
  in remembrance of his mercy,
according to the promise he made to our
    ancestors,
  to Abraham and to his descendants for ever.'
And Mary remained with Elizabeth for about three
months and then returned to her home.

• Mary's song of praise before the birth of Jesus
echoes the song of Hannah after the birth of
Samuel (1 Samuel 2:1–10). They were grateful to
God, as was Elizabeth, for the gifts given to them

in their children. May we have grateful hearts that exude joy and hope in recognising the love and mercy God has shown us. Perhaps we might write our own song of praise.

- We are shown a God of reversals, who has scattered the proud in their thoughts and hearts, brought down the powerful and lifted up the lowly. God looked with favour on Mary, a lowly servant. We pray for humble hearts that can acknowledge the many ways in which God has gifted us in life.

Saturday 23 December
Luke 1:57–66

Now the time came for Elizabeth to give birth, and she bore a son. Her neighbours and relatives heard that the Lord had shown his great mercy to her, and they rejoiced with her.

On the eighth day they came to circumcise the child, and they were going to name him Zechariah after his father. But his mother said, 'No; he is to be called John.' They said to her, 'None of your relatives has this name.' Then they began motioning to his father to find out what name he wanted to give him. He asked for a writing-tablet and wrote, 'His name is John.' And all of them were amazed. Immediately his mouth was opened and his tongue freed, and he began to speak, praising God. Fear came over all their neighbours, and all these things were talked about throughout the entire hill country of Judea. All who heard them pondered them and said, 'What then will this child become?' For, indeed, the hand of the Lord was with him.

- The birth of John was an important family occasion for Elizabeth and Zechariah. Elizabeth verified the name and Zechariah had to write it on a tablet before his speech returned. We pray that we who are named may have our mouths opened and our tongues freed, so that we can give further praise to God.

- The birth of John was more than a local celebration. Neighbours and relatives rejoiced with Elizabeth and Zechariah, but what happened was talked about throughout the entire hill country of Judea. It heralded a bigger picture in the unfolding of God's story of salvation. We pray that we may have a better sense of community and share good news in our support of each other.

The Fourth Week of Advent/Christmas

24–30 December 2023

Something to think and pray about each day this week:

Many looked forward to the coming of the Messiah, the Christ. He was the hope of the ages to come. But they were dead and gone when he arrived. Jesus praises us that we have seen him. We have seen in him the image of God. As Victor Hugo wrote in *Les Misérables*, if you love, you have seen the face of God. The Jesus we await now is the Jesus we can meet every day – in love, in prayer and in the Eucharist. This is what Pope Francis calls 'social love'. Social love includes our daily relationships, our families and friends, but it also goes beyond them to include a love for the whole world, especially for the poor and those who live in worlds of injustice, war and violence. Our preparation for Christmas puts many challenges to us. The needs of people, both near and far, are great. In Advent we lean into our greatest longings and into the greatest needs of the whole world.

Donal Neary SJ,
The Messenger Advent Booklet:
Reflections on the Daily Readings

The Presence of God

'Come to me, all you who are weary and are carrying heavy burdens, and I will give you rest.' Here I am, Lord. I come to seek your presence. I long for your healing power.

Freedom

'In these days, God taught me as a schoolteacher teaches a pupil' (St Ignatius).

I remind myself that there are things God has to teach me yet, and I ask for the grace to hear those things and let them change me.

Consciousness

Help me, Lord, to be more conscious of your presence. Teach me to recognise your presence in others.

Fill my heart with gratitude for the times your love has been shown to me through the care of others.

The Word

God speaks to each of us individually. I listen attentively to hear what he is saying to me. Read the text a few times, then listen. *(Please turn to the Scripture on the following pages. Inspiration points are there, should you need them. When you are ready, return here to continue.)*

Conversation

Conversation requires talking and listening.

As I talk to Jesus, may I also learn to be still and listen.

I picture the gentleness in his eyes and the smile full of love as he gazes on me.

I can be totally honest with Jesus as I tell him of my worries and my cares.

I will open my heart to him as I tell him of my fears and my doubts.

I will ask him to help me place myself fully in his care and to abandon myself to him, knowing that he always wants what is best for me.

Conclusion

I thank God for these moments we have spent together and for any insights I have been given concerning the text.

Sunday 24 December
Fourth Sunday of Advent
Luke 1:26–38

In the sixth month the angel Gabriel was sent by God to a town in Galilee called Nazareth, to a virgin engaged to a man whose name was Joseph, of the house of David. The virgin's name was Mary. And he came to her and said, 'Greetings, favoured one! The Lord is with you.' But she was much perplexed by his words and pondered what sort of greeting this might be. The angel said to her, 'Do not be afraid, Mary, for you have found favour with God. And now, you will conceive in your womb and bear a son, and you will name him Jesus. He will be great, and will be called the Son of the Most High, and the Lord God will give to him the throne of his ancestor David. He will reign over the house of Jacob for ever, and of his kingdom there will be no end.' Mary said to the angel, 'How can this be, since I am a virgin?' The angel said to her, 'The Holy Spirit will come upon you, and the power of the Most High will overshadow you; therefore the child to be born will be holy; he will be called Son of God. And now, your relative Elizabeth in her old age has also conceived a son; and this is the sixth month for her who was said to be barren. For nothing will be impossible with God.' Then Mary said, 'Here am I, the servant of the Lord; let it be with me according to your word.' Then the angel departed from her.

- There is a phrase with a familiar ring to it: 'Do not be afraid, for you have found favour with God.' Being asked to do something different can evoke such a response. However, God's love and fidelity were assured, so it can be said: 'Remember that the power behind you is greater than the task ahead.' May we have the faith to rely on God and not be caught out by our own limited resources.
- Mary was told that all would happen through the action of the Holy Spirit. The name and mission of Jesus as Son of the most High whose kingdom will not end was stated clearly. We pray to imitate Mary in our sharing of that mission.

Monday 25 December
The Nativity of the Lord
John 1:1–18

In the beginning was the Word, and the Word was with God, and the Word was God. He was in the beginning with God. All things came into being through him, and without him not one thing came into being. What has come into being in him was life, and the life was the light of all people. The light shines in the darkness, and the darkness did not overcome it.

There was a man sent from God, whose name was John. He came as a witness to testify to the light, so that all might believe through him. He himself was not the light, but he came to testify to the light. The true light, which enlightens everyone, was coming into the world.

He was in the world, and the world came into being through him; yet the world did not know him. He came to what was his own, and his own people did not accept him. But to all who received him, who believed in his name, he gave power to become children of God, who were born, not of blood or of the will of the flesh or of the will of man, but of God.

And the Word became flesh and lived among us, and we have seen his glory, the glory as of a father's only son, full of grace and truth. (John testified to him and cried out, 'This was he of whom I said, "He who comes after me ranks ahead of me because he was before me."') From his fullness we have all received, grace upon grace. The law indeed was given through Moses; grace and truth came through Jesus Christ. No one has ever seen God. It is God the only Son, who is close to the Father's heart, who has made him known.

- Christmas celebrates the Word made flesh. We share in the divinity of him who shared our humanity. It is a new beginning, re-echoing the creation story in

Genesis. The Word was the light of all people. In the darkness of our lives and world we turn to Jesus, the light, and pray that he may help us to overcome the darkness and give witness to his presence.

- Jesus is the Word uttered by the Father to give us new life. The living word of scripture helps us to know Jesus better. May our words be in harmony with the words of scripture in proclaiming the Eternal Word as our good news of salvation.

Tuesday 26 December
St Stephen, Martyr
Matthew 10:17–22

Jesus said to his disciples, 'Beware of them, for they will hand you over to councils and flog you in their synagogues; and you will be dragged before governors and kings because of me, as a testimony to them and the Gentiles. When they hand you over, do not worry about how you are to speak or what you are to say; for what you are to say will be given to you at that time; for it is not you who speak, but the Spirit of your Father speaking through you. Brother will betray brother to death, and a father his child, and children will rise against parents and have them put to death; and you will be hated by all because of my name. But the one who endures to the end will be saved.'

- We are brought down to earth from any romantic notion of yesterday with the death of Stephen. All would not welcome Jesus – there will be opposition and persecution. There will be betrayal by a member of his inner circle. Give us the grace to face the misunderstandings and challenges of discipleship.

- Stephen relied on God. We are not to worry about what to say as that will be given, with the Spirit of the Father speaking through us. May we have the faith and courage to endure the challenges and temptations of life.

Wednesday 27 December
St John, Apostle and Evangelist
John 20:1a.2–8

Early on the first day of the week, while it was still dark, Mary Magdalene came to the tomb and saw that the stone had been removed from the tomb. So she ran and went to Simon Peter and the other disciple, the one whom Jesus loved, and said to them, 'They have taken the Lord out of the tomb, and we do not know where they have laid him.' Then Peter and the other disciple set out and went towards the tomb. The two were running together, but the other disciple outran Peter and reached the tomb first. He bent down to look in and saw the linen wrappings lying there, but he did not go in. Then Simon Peter came, following him, and went into the tomb. He saw the linen wrappings lying there, and the cloth that had been on Jesus' head, not lying with the linen wrappings but rolled up in a place by itself. Then the other disciple, who reached the tomb first, also went in, and he saw and believed.

- John is understood to be 'the disciple Jesus loved'. He was reclining next to Jesus at the Last Supper when the question of betrayal came up (John 13:24–25); he was present at the foot of the cross and promised to take care of Mary after it (John 19:2–27). We pray, through his intercession, to know, love, welcome and serve Jesus.

- Mary Magdalene ran to tell Peter and John and they ran together to the tomb. John deferred to Peter when they arrived, but he was the more intuitive one in coming to an understanding of and belief in what happened. May we draw strength from his example and be able to slow down so that we can come to a deeper appreciation of the new life Jesus brings.

Thursday 28 December
The Holy Innocents
Matthew 2:13–18

Now after they had left, an angel of the Lord appeared to Joseph in a dream and said, 'Get up, take the child and his mother, and flee to Egypt, and remain there until I tell you; for Herod is about to search for the child, to destroy him.' Then Joseph got up, took the child and his mother by night, and went to Egypt, and remained there until the death of Herod. This was to fulfil what had been spoken by the Lord through the prophet, 'Out of Egypt I have called my son.'

When Herod saw that he had been tricked by the wise men, he was infuriated, and he sent and killed all the children in and around Bethlehem who were two years old or under, according to the time that he had learned from the wise men. Then was fulfilled what had been spoken through the prophet Jeremiah:

'A voice was heard in Ramah,
  wailing and loud lamentation,
Rachel weeping for her children;
  she refused to be consoled, because they are
    no more.'

- From early on, there was opposition to Jesus and what he came to do. The seeds of the passion were evident already. To King Herod, the child Jesus was a threat, a potential opponent. This feast gives some preparation for what lay ahead, when others would seek Jesus' death. May we learn from those who showed love and care for Jesus so that we value all children of God.

- We live at a time when there are many child victims of abuse, of trafficking, of exploitation and wars. May we cherish children as God's gift and learn to maintain a childlike trust in you, Lord, to guide us in our relationships with them, so that they are safe.

Friday 29 December
Luke 2:22–35

When the time came for their purification according to the law of Moses, they brought him up to Jerusalem to present him to the Lord (as it is written in the law of the Lord, 'Every firstborn male shall be designated as holy to the Lord'), and they offered a sacrifice according to what is stated in the law of the Lord, 'a pair of turtle-doves or two young pigeons.'

Now there was a man in Jerusalem whose name was Simeon; this man was righteous and devout, looking forward to the consolation of Israel, and the Holy Spirit rested on him. It had been revealed to him by the Holy Spirit that he would not see death before he had seen the Lord's Messiah. Guided by the Spirit, Simeon came into the temple; and when the parents brought in the child Jesus, to do for him what was customary under the law, Simeon took him in his arms and praised God, saying,

'Master, now you are dismissing your servant in
       peace,
   according to your word;
for my eyes have seen your salvation,
   which you have prepared in the presence of all
       peoples,
a light for revelation to the Gentiles
   and for glory to your people Israel.'

And the child's father and mother were amazed at what was being said about him. Then Simeon blessed them and said to his mother Mary, 'This child is destined for the falling and the rising of many in Israel, and to be a sign that will be opposed so that the inner thoughts of many will be revealed – and a sword will pierce your own soul too.'

- Jesus was named eight days after his birth and then, after forty days, he was presented in the Temple. All this was in accordance with Jewish tradition. Jesus was referred to as the promised Messiah, who would redeem Israel. May we draw fruit from that event, recognising the role of the past, but ask for openness to the future the Lord promised.
- Simeon was righteous and devout and looked forward to the consolation of Israel. He was an older person who was familiar with the faith story of his people, but he also knew of the promised Saviour. We pray for that faith vision that helps us know what is valuable but remain open to what the Lord reveals to us.

Saturday 30 December
Luke 2:36–40

There was also a prophet, Anna the daughter of Phanuel, of the tribe of Asher. She was of a great age, having lived with her husband for seven years after her marriage, then as a widow to the age of eighty-four. She never left the temple but worshipped there with fasting and prayer night and day. At that moment she came, and began to praise God and to speak about the child to all who were looking for the redemption of Jerusalem.

When they had finished everything required by the law of the Lord, they returned to Galilee, to their own town of Nazareth. The child grew and became strong, filled with wisdom; and the favour of God was upon him.

- Anna was an aged woman who was widowed soon after her marriage. She was from a little-known northern tribe. The qualities of her life, her commitment to prayer and to the temple speak eloquently of her. In the ordinariness of our lives, may we have the same faith to wait and to recognise Jesus in the ways he comes into our lives.

- Anna's life could not have been easy, but she had come to terms with it. She was not looking back in self-pity or regret. Rather, she could praise God and speak about Jesus to all who were looking for the redemption of Jerusalem. Lord, you call us beyond the struggles of the past and offer us hope for what lies ahead. May the example of Anna inspire us to live in that spirit.

The First Week of Christmas

31 December 2023–6 January 2024

Something to think and pray about each day this week:

Most cribs have an open door. This is God's door: it is never closed to us. An important message to us today is welcoming and openness. The bonds of Christmas are strong; of memories, love, faith, grief and hope. We remember that with each other we meet and we share life – we grow together.

Bonds can be strong or limited. The bond with a cousin to whom we send a card is not as active a bond as the family we meet regularly and help, support and love. We meet at funerals and weddings. Better that, however, than never meeting at all. Bonds can renew love, even if there are blocks to our relationship. Bonds are made up of love and quarrels, attractions and histories, of all sorts of good and bad things. Even the person who does not go home for Christmas thinks of home these days. Our Christian faith may be a bond. Christmas faith may be a bit like 'we only meet at Christmas'! Isn't it good we meet at Christmas and strengthen these bonds among us? Bonds of love, family, neighbourhood and faith. Something of God, and the community of the Church, binds us this time of year.

We find that God is close and near, and that his word involves us with others – especially with the poor and the migrant, the sinner and the saint. All are called together in him. We visit the poor infant born on the side of the road to make us remember at other times that many are born like that today, that many are poor, and many need the drastic help which Mary and Joseph needed that night.

Give thanks for the good Christmases and ask
help for any painful memories to place in the crib.
O come let us adore him.

Donal Neary SJ,
Gospel Reflections for Sundays of Year B

The Presence of God

'I am standing at the door, knocking,' says the Lord. What a wonderful privilege that the Lord of all creation desires to come to me. I welcome his presence.

Freedom

Leave me here freely all alone. / In cell where never sunlight shone. / Should no one ever speak to me. / This golden silence makes me free!

—Part of a poem written by a prisoner at Dachau concentration camp

Consciousness

How am I really feeling? Lighthearted? Heavy-hearted? I may be very much at peace, happy to be here. Equally, I may be frustrated, worried or angry. I acknowledge how I really am. It is the real me whom the Lord loves.

The Word

I take my time to read the word of God slowly, a few times, allowing myself to dwell on anything that strikes me. *(Please turn to the Scripture on the following pages. Inspiration points are there, should you need them. When you are ready, return here to continue.)*

Conversation

Do I notice myself reacting as I pray with the word of God? Do I feel challenged, comforted, angry? Imagining Jesus sitting or standing by me, I speak out my feelings, as one trusted friend to another.

Conclusion

Glory be to the Father, and to the Son, and to the Holy Spirit,
As it was in the beginning, is now and ever shall be,
World without end. Amen.

Sunday 31 December
The Holy Family
Luke 2:22–40

When the time came for their purification according to the law of Moses, they brought him up to Jerusalem to present him to the Lord (as it is written in the law of the Lord, 'Every firstborn male shall be designated as holy to the Lord'), and they offered a sacrifice according to what is stated in the law of the Lord, 'a pair of turtle-doves or two young pigeons.'

Now there was a man in Jerusalem whose name was Simeon; this man was righteous and devout, looking forward to the consolation of Israel, and the Holy Spirit rested on him. It had been revealed to him by the Holy Spirit that he would not see death before he had seen the Lord's Messiah. Guided by the Spirit, Simeon came into the temple; and when the parents brought in the child Jesus, to do for him what was customary under the law, Simeon took him in his arms and praised God, saying,

'Master, now you are dismissing your servant in
    peace,
  according to your word;
for my eyes have seen your salvation,
  which you have prepared in the presence of all
    peoples,
a light for revelation to the Gentiles
  and for glory to your people Israel.'

And the child's father and mother were amazed at what was being said about him. Then Simeon blessed them and said to his mother Mary, 'This child is destined for the falling and the rising of many in Israel, and to be a sign that will be opposed so that the inner thoughts of many will be revealed – and a sword will pierce your own soul too.'

There was also a prophet, Anna the daughter of Phanuel, of the tribe of Asher. She was of a great age, having lived with her husband for seven years after her marriage, then as a widow to the age of eighty-four. She never left the temple but worshipped there with fasting and prayer night and day. At that moment she came, and began to praise God and to speak about the child to all who were looking for the redemption of Jerusalem.

When they had finished everything required by the law of the Lord, they returned to Galilee, to their own town of Nazareth. The child grew and became strong, filled with wisdom; and the favour of God was upon him.

• We had Zechariah and Elizabeth, Mary and Joseph, and Simeon and Anna, though the latter were not a couple as such. All shared a vision and were open to God's ways. Jesus was central. Mary and Joseph took Jesus to the temple and made their offering as they were a family of faith. We pray for the wisdom to live our faith and present Jesus to others as a guide in life.

- Life in a quiet village such as Nazareth was ordinary in many ways. Jesus grew and became strong. He was maturing in faith as well as humanly, for he was 'filled with wisdom and the favour of God was upon him'. May we continue to grow in maturity, both humanly and spiritually.

Monday 1 January
Mary, Mother of God
Luke 2:16–21

So they went with haste and found Mary and Joseph, and the child lying in the manger. When they saw this, they made known what had been told them about this child; and all who heard it were amazed at what the shepherds told them. But Mary treasured all these words and pondered them in her heart. The shepherds returned, glorifying and praising God for all they had heard and seen, as it had been told them.

After eight days had passed, it was time to circumcise the child; and he was called Jesus, the name given by the angel before he was conceived in the womb.

- A new year has begun. Mary helped initiate a new era in giving birth to Jesus, the Son of God, the promised Messiah. The divine met the human and she was a willing recipient of God's will for her. May we bring forth new life and share it generously in her spirit to the glory of her Son.

- Mary said 'yes' to a way of life. What lay ahead had an element of mystery to it. We are told that she was amazed at what was being said about Jesus. She pondered and wondered. Inspired by the shepherds, we ask to be open to God's mysterious ways and to take time to ponder and pray on them.

Tuesday 2 January
John 1:19–28

This is the testimony given by John when the Jews sent priests and Levites from Jerusalem to ask him, 'Who are you?' He confessed and did not deny it, but confessed, 'I am not the Messiah.' And they asked him, 'What then? Are you Elijah?' He said, 'I am not.' 'Are you the prophet?' He answered, 'No.' Then they said to him, 'Who are you? Let us have an answer for those who sent us. What do you say about yourself?' He said,

'I am the voice of one crying out in the
    wilderness,
"Make straight the way of the Lord",'
as the prophet Isaiah said.

Now they had been sent from the Pharisees. They asked him, 'Why then are you baptising if you are neither the Messiah, nor Elijah, nor the prophet?' John answered them, 'I baptise with water. Among you stands one whom you do not know, the one who is coming after me; I am not worthy to untie the thong of his sandal.' This took place in Bethany across the Jordan where John was baptising.

- Witnesses give evidence. John the Baptist bore testimony by his words and actions. While he was a prophet, he was distinctive in how he lived in the time and setting of his ministry. May our lives bear witness to our faith in Jesus in this time and may our words be in harmony with it.
- Knowing Jesus is at the heart of our call. It looks to a personal relationship, not just information about Jesus. We pray for the humility of John to recognise and accept our role and for the freedom to live it.

Wednesday 3 January
John 1:29–34
The next day he saw Jesus coming towards him and declared, 'Here is the Lamb of God who takes away the sin of the world! This is he of whom I said, "After me comes a man who ranks ahead of me because he was before me." I myself did not know him; but I came baptising with water for this reason, that he might be revealed to Israel.' And John testified, 'I saw the Spirit descending from heaven like a dove, and it remained on him. I myself did not know him, but the one who sent me to baptise with water said to me, "He on whom you see the Spirit descend and remain

is the one who baptises with the Holy Spirit." And I myself have seen and have testified that this is the Son of God.'

- John could declare that Jesus was the Lamb of God who takes away the sin of the world. John's mission was preparatory and the focus was now beginning to shift to Jesus and the baptism he offered. Lord, may we draw strength from the example of John and make Jesus the centre of our attention and prayer.
- John desired that Jesus be revealed as the promised one. The presence and action of the Spirit was giving testimony to who Jesus was. We ask for a deeper faith in Jesus as our saviour and desire to bear witness to him as the Lamb of God.

Thursday 4 January
John 1:35–42

The next day John again was standing with two of his disciples, and as he watched Jesus walk by, he exclaimed, 'Look, here is the Lamb of God!' The two disciples heard him say this, and they followed Jesus. When Jesus turned and saw them following, he said to them, 'What are you looking for?' They said to him, 'Rabbi' (which translated means Teacher), 'where are you staying?' He said to them, 'Come and see.' They came and saw where he was staying, and they remained with him that day. It was about four o'clock in the afternoon. One of the two who heard John speak and followed him was Andrew, Simon Peter's brother. He first found his brother Simon and said to him, 'We have found the Messiah' (which is translated Anointed). He brought Simon to Jesus, who looked at him and said, 'You are Simon son of John. You are to be called Cephas' (which is translated Peter).

- Again, John referred to Jesus as the Lamb of God. Two of his disciples decided to follow Jesus who asked them what they wanted. He invited them to 'come and see'. We do not know what they talked about but they spent the rest of the day with Jesus. Lord, let our desires bring us to come and see, to spend time with Jesus, so that we can learn more about him and what he wants for us.

- Word began to spread, with Andrew introducing his brother to the Lord. Jesus gave Simon a new name, for a new mission. We remember those who introduced us to Jesus in a personal way and give thanks for them.

Friday 5 January
John 1:43–51

The next day Jesus decided to go to Galilee. He found Philip and said to him, 'Follow me.' Now Philip was from Bethsaida, the city of Andrew and

Peter. Philip found Nathanael and said to him, 'We have found him about whom Moses in the law and also the prophets wrote, Jesus son of Joseph from Nazareth.' Nathanael said to him, 'Can anything good come out of Nazareth?' Philip said to him, 'Come and see.' When Jesus saw Nathanael coming towards him, he said of him, 'Here is truly an Israelite in whom there is no deceit!' Nathanael asked him, 'Where did you come to know me?' Jesus answered, 'I saw you under the fig tree before Philip called you.' Nathanael replied, 'Rabbi, you are the Son of God! You are the King of Israel!' Jesus answered, 'Do you believe because I told you that I saw you under the fig tree? You will see greater things than these.' And he said to him, 'Very truly, I tell you, you will see heaven opened and the angels of God ascending and descending upon the Son of Man.'

- More people were introduced to Jesus. There was discussion as to who he was. Human considerations, such as background, could get in the way for some. Lord, you came in the flesh into the ordinary but desire us to embrace the new life you offer.

- Jesus was presenting something at a deeper level, beyond the practical. His message and promise was at a spiritual or faith level. May we grow in openness to 'see greater things' that will reveal the Lord more fully to us.

Saturday 6 January
The Epiphany of Our Lord (IRL)
Matthew 2:1–12

In the time of King Herod, after Jesus was born in Bethlehem of Judea, wise men from the East came to Jerusalem, asking, 'Where is the child who has been born king of the Jews? For we observed his star at its rising, and have come to pay him homage.' When King Herod heard this, he was frightened, and all Jerusalem with him; and calling together all the chief priests and scribes of the people, he inquired of them where the Messiah was to be born. They told him, 'In Bethlehem of Judea; for so it has been written by the prophet:

"And you, Bethlehem, in the land of Judah,
   are by no means least among the rulers of
      Judah;
for from you shall come a ruler
   who is to shepherd my people Israel."'

Then Herod secretly called for the wise men and learned from them the exact time when the star had appeared. Then he sent them to Bethlehem, saying, 'Go and search diligently for the child; and when you have found him, bring me word so that I may also go and pay him homage.' When they had heard the king, they set out; and there, ahead of them, went the star that they had seen at its rising, until it stopped over the place where the child was. When they saw that the star had stopped, they were overwhelmed with joy. On entering the house, they saw the child with Mary his mother; and they knelt down and paid him homage. Then, opening their treasure-chests, they offered him gifts of gold, frankincense, and myrrh. And having been warned in a dream not to return to Herod, they left for their own country by another road.

- Simeon said Jesus was 'a light for revelation to the Gentiles' (Luke 1:32). The arrival of the wise men was an epiphany, a manifestation of Jesus as Saviour of all. King Herod wanted to safeguard his own interests. Jesus is our star, guiding us to life. May we have the faith to follow him and to manifest him to others.

- A king was afraid of a child. Herod saw Jesus in earthly terms as a potential opponent, thus his search was devious. In his words, may we 'go and search diligently for the child', so that we may offer true homage to him as our king.

The Second Week of Christmas

7–13 January 2024

Something to think and pray about each day this week:

I love wood with a good back story. I made three crosses from wood I rescued from a rubbish tip. They are from a Paper Birch tree that had received a bit of a trim. The tree is in the old Poor Clare Convent in Belfast (I work on the site).

Having rescued the rather nondescript lump of wood I set about sawing it open and saw these wonderful patterns and grain. It really is one of the most beautiful pieces of wood I've ever worked with. And it teaches me a lesson: what is thrown away or discounted as rubbish is often precious.

This applies even more to people than wood. Many people are marginalised, discriminated against and consigned to the rubbish tip of life. And yet all people are precious. Inside all of us we are just as beautiful as and more than the wood my three crosses are made of.

Jesus often hung around with those consigned to the rubbish tip – those seen as 'less than' or on the outside. I think he sends us a powerful lesson down through time – we are all one. No one is on the outside.

Jim Deeds,
The Sacred Heart Messenger, October 2020

The Presence of God

As I sit here, the beating of my heart,
the ebb and flow of my breathing, the movements of my mind
are all signs of God's ongoing creation of me.
I pause for a moment and become aware
of this presence of God within me.

Freedom

Everything has the potential to draw from me a fuller love and life.
Yet my desires are often fixed, caught, on illusions of fulfilment.
I ask that God, through my freedom, may orchestrate my desires in a vibrant loving melody rich in harmony.

Consciousness

I ask, how am I within myself today? Am I particularly tired, stressed or off-form? If any of these characteristics apply, can I try to let go of the concerns that disturb me?

The Word

I read the word of God slowly, a few times over, and I listen to what God is saying to me. *(Please turn to the Scripture on the following pages. Inspiration points are there, should you need them. When you are ready, return here to continue.)*

Conversation

I begin to talk with Jesus about the Scripture I have just read. What part of it strikes a chord in me? Perhaps the words of a friend or a story I have heard recently will slowly rise to the surface of my consciousness. If so, does the story throw light on what the Scripture passage may be trying to say to me?

Conclusion

Glory be to the Father, and to the Son, and to the Holy Spirit,
As it was in the beginning, is now and ever shall be,
World without end. Amen.

Sunday 7 January

The Baptism of Our Lord (IRL) The Epiphany of Our Lord (USA)

Mark 1:7–11

He proclaimed, 'The one who is more powerful than I is coming after me; I am not worthy to stoop down and untie the thong of his sandals. I have baptised you with water; but he will baptise you with the Holy Spirit.'

In those days Jesus came from Nazareth of Galilee and was baptised by John in the Jordan. And just as he was coming up out of the water, he saw the heavens torn apart and the Spirit descending like a dove on him. And a voice came from heaven, 'You are my Son, the Beloved; with you I am well pleased.'

- John the Baptist was clear about his identity and his role, which was to prepare the way for Jesus. His baptism was one of repentance. In our baptism, we are immersed in Jesus' mission and given new life. We pray that we may introduce Jesus, help make him known and give him the primary place in our lives.

- At his baptism, Jesus was given heavenly approval with the presence of the Spirit and the voice of the Father. Jesus was about to embark on his mission. He was the beloved Son in whom the Father was pleased. In baptism, we are made beloved children; we pray that we may appreciate the gift Jesus shares with us, so that we may live our calling in a generous spirit.

Monday 8 January
The Baptism of Our Lord (USA)
Mark 1:14–20

Now after John was arrested, Jesus came to Galilee, proclaiming the good news of God, and saying, 'The time is fulfilled, and the kingdom of God has come near; repent, and believe in the good news.' As Jesus passed along the Sea of Galilee, he saw Simon and his brother Andrew casting a net into the sea – for they were fishermen. And Jesus said to them, 'Follow me and I will make you fish for people.' And immediately they left their nets and followed him. As he went a little farther, he saw James son of Zebedee and his brother John, who were in their boat mending the nets. Immediately he called them; and they left their father Zebedee in the boat with the hired men, and followed him.

• The beginning of Jesus' mission of proclaiming good news took place at a time and in a context. His call to repentance asked for a change of life, reminding his hearers that the kingdom of God was near. The same invitation is given to us now. May we allow his word and kingdom to find a home in our hearts.

• Ordinary people were called from their places of work and they gave a ready response. The implications of the decision would become more apparent in due course, but their initial generosity was important to begin with. May we have that generosity in hearing and responding to the Lord's call to us now.

Tuesday 9 January
Mark 1:21–28

They went to Capernaum; and when the sabbath came, he entered the synagogue and taught. They were astounded at his teaching, for he taught them as one having authority, and not as the scribes. Just then there was in their synagogue a man with an unclean spirit, and he cried out, 'What have you to do with us, Jesus of Nazareth? Have you come to destroy us? I know who you are, the Holy One of God.' But Jesus rebuked him, saying, 'Be silent, and come out of him!' And the unclean spirit, throwing him into convulsions and crying with a loud voice, came out of him. They were all amazed, and they kept on asking one another, 'What is this? A new teaching – with authority! He commands even the unclean spirits, and they obey him.' At once his fame began to spread throughout the surrounding region of Galilee.

• Jesus took sabbath time, going to the synagogue to teach. He made an impression on those present. He was giving example as well as spiritual nourishment to his hearers. Lord, give us ears to hear your word, which is ever new. May it may strengthen us in following you.

• It was an unclean spirit who recognised Jesus for who he was, calling him the Holy One of God. The power of Jesus was greater and he cast the spirit out. Lord, give us the wisdom to rely on you in the challenges that we face in life, especially when they seem too strong to deal with.

Wednesday 10 January
Mark 1:29–39

As soon as they left the synagogue, they entered the house of Simon and Andrew, with James and John. Now Simon's mother-in-law was in bed with a fever, and they told him about her at once. He came and took her by the hand and lifted her up. Then the fever left her, and she began to serve them.

That evening, at sunset, they brought to him all who were sick or possessed with demons. And the whole city was gathered around the door. And he cured many who were sick with various diseases, and cast out many demons; and he would not permit the demons to speak, because they knew him.

In the morning, while it was still very dark, he got up and went out to a deserted place, and there he prayed. And Simon and his companions hunted for him. When they found him, they said to him, 'Everyone is searching for you.' He answered, 'Let us go on to the neighbouring towns, so that I may proclaim the message there also; for that is what I came out to do.' And he went throughout Galilee, proclaiming the message in their synagogues and casting out demons.

• Simon's mother-in-law must have been a prominent member of the community, given the promptness with which Jesus was told and the immediacy of his response. It tells us that healing leads to service. May Jesus take us by the hand and raise us up to serve others in his name.

- In a busy life, Jesus took quiet time for prayer. Then he indicated that he wanted to move on when his companions found him and wanted him to go back. Lord, give us the freedom to see beyond the immediate need, especially when there is something more urgent to be met.

Thursday 11 January
Mark 1:40–45

A leper came to him begging him, and kneeling he said to him, 'If you choose, you can make me clean.' Moved with pity, Jesus stretched out his hand and touched him, and said to him, 'I do choose. Be made clean!' Immediately the leprosy left him, and he was made clean. After sternly warning him he sent him away at once, saying to him, 'See that you say nothing to anyone; but go, show yourself to the priest, and offer for your cleansing what Moses commanded, as a testimony to them.' But he went out and began to proclaim it freely, and to spread the word, so that Jesus could no longer go into a town openly, but stayed out in the country; and people came to him from every quarter.

- A leper begged Jesus to be cured. His desire met the desire of Jesus for him. Jesus wanted to be known as more than a miracle worker, so he asked the man to be quiet. May we have the courage and humility to bring our desires to the Lord and allow him to transform them so that they are more in harmony with his desires for us.

- The leper needed a health certificate from a priest to verify his healing. Jesus got more publicity than he desired and tried to isolate himself, but people continued to come to him. Lord, you offer us inner healing but desire us to draw people to you. May we have the clarity to ask and the freedom to accept what you provide for us.

Friday 12 January
Mark 2:1–12

When he returned to Capernaum after some days, it was reported that he was at home. So many gathered around that there was no longer room for them, not even in front of the door; and he was speaking the word to them. Then some people came, bringing to him a paralysed man, carried by four of them. And when they could not bring him to Jesus because of the crowd, they removed the roof above him; and after having dug through it, they let down the mat on which the paralytic lay. When Jesus saw their faith, he said to the paralytic, 'Son, your sins are forgiven.' Now some of the scribes were sitting there, questioning in their hearts, 'Why does this fellow speak in this way? It is blasphemy! Who can forgive sins but God alone?' At once Jesus perceived in his spirit that they were discussing these questions among themselves; and he said to them, 'Why do you raise such questions in your hearts? Which is easier, to say to the paralytic, "Your sins are forgiven", or to say, "Stand up and take your mat and walk"? But so that you may know that the Son of Man has authority on earth to forgive sins' – he said to the paralytic – 'I say to you, stand up, take your mat and go to your home.' And he stood up, and immediately took the mat and went out before all of them; so that they were all amazed and glorified God, saying, 'We have never seen anything like this!'

• The return of Jesus attracted a crowd. The paralytic needed help. The people were creative in their approach and were able to place the man in front of Jesus. May we have creativity in coming to Jesus and have the freedom to accept the help of others to facilitate this.

• Jesus had concern for the whole person. He began with interior healing, with the forgiveness of sins. This challenged those present, but then, to the amazement of all, he cured the paralytic. Lord, give us a greater faith in you to accept your healing, internal and external, that we may praise you more fully as our Lord.

Saturday 13 January
Mark 2:13–17

Jesus went out again beside the lake; the whole crowd gathered around him, and he taught them. As he was walking along, he saw Levi son of Alphaeus sitting at the tax booth, and he said to him, 'Follow me.' And he got up and followed him.

And as he sat at dinner in Levi's house, many tax-collectors and sinners were also sitting with Jesus and his disciples – for there were many who followed him. When the scribes of the Pharisees saw that he was eating with sinners and tax-collectors, they said to his disciples, 'Why does he eat with tax-collectors and sinners?' When Jesus heard this, he said to them, 'Those who are well have no need of a physician, but those who are sick; I have come to call not the righteous but sinners.'

- This is a different call, as Levi was summoned from his tax booth to follow Jesus. Another strange choice and an unusual setting, but it was the Lord's choice. Lord, you have called us as other surprising choices. Give us the grace to respond with gratitude so that we may follow you more closely.
- Jesus befriended outsiders and was at home with them. They were people who could recognise their need, in contrast to the scribes and the Pharisees. Lord, we are the tax collectors and sinners whom you have invited to share table with you. Let us accept your invitation with gratitude and grow in openness to what you offer to us.

Sacred Space

An Advent Retreat

Introduction

There's a lot of waiting in Advent – four weeks of waiting for all the celebrations of Christmas. There's longing, too, and wondering, longing for the coming of the Lord and wondering what it means that this year Jesus will be born again among us. There's sadness as we remember those who have shared Christmas with us and have gone home to God before us. There's also the memory of Christmas in family, with community, remembering the absent ones we miss a lot this time of year. It's a time of personal and community richness, of engagement with the Lord in faith. We are allowing the mystery of the coming of the Lord to engage us and deepen our faith and love.

The spirit of Christmas is near in so many ways and we can allow everything of Christmas – the street decorations, the parties, the gifts and everything else remind us always of the true meaning: God is with us, Emmanuel. We hear people say, 'Put

Christ back into Christmas' – we can find Christ in everything of Christmas.

The Advent readings remind us often of the poor of the world, and of those who need God in their search for meaning, hope and love in life.

Our faith can become real once it touches our heart, our soul, our spirit and our whole being, once it allows God to be born and reborn in the manger of our heart; once we let the star of Bethlehem guide us to the place where the Son of God lies, not among kings and riches, but among the poor and humble. 'It depends solely on you. Ah, if only your heart could become a manger, then God would once again become a child on this earth' (*Angelus Silesius*).

SESSION 1

Invitation to Stillness

As you begin this time of prayer, allow your body to settle into a peaceful and comfortable position. Let your mind settle, putting your preoccupations into God's hands for this time. Listen to the sounds around you, focusing in from those far away to those nearest to you: the sounds within your room, the sound of your own breathing, relaxing as you hear each breath drawn.

Reading

Isaiah 11:1–10

A shoot shall come out from the stock of Jesse,
   and a branch shall grow out of his roots.
The spirit of the Lord shall rest on him,
   the spirit of wisdom and understanding,
   the spirit of counsel and might,
   the spirit of knowledge and the fear of
      the Lord.
His delight shall be in the fear of the Lord.

He shall not judge by what his eyes see,
   or decide by what his ears hear;
but with righteousness he shall judge the poor,
   and decide with equity for the meek of the
      earth;

he shall strike the earth with the rod of his
      mouth,
   and with the breath of his lips he shall kill the
      wicked.
Righteousness shall be the belt around his
      waist,
   and faithfulness the belt around his loins.

The wolf shall live with the lamb,
   the leopard shall lie down with the kid,
the calf and the lion and the fatling together,
   and a little child shall lead them.
The cow and the bear shall graze,
   their young shall lie down together;
   and the lion shall eat straw like the ox.
The nursing child shall play over the hole of the
      asp,
   and the weaned child shall put its hand on the
      adder's den.
They will not hurt or destroy
   on all my holy mountain;
for the earth will be full of the knowledge of
      the Lord
   as the waters cover the sea.
On that day the root of Jesse shall stand as a signal to
the peoples; the nations shall inquire of him, and his
dwelling shall be glorious.

Reflect

We often look forward to having a good time. We hope that a party or holiday will be the best ever. Today's reading from the Book of Isaiah is about the news that God's people were going to have a good time. A person would arrive who would be wise, understanding, powerful and just. This good time would bring peace for all; even the animals would lie down together, and violence would end. Advent brings out our best hopes for our families, localities, countries and indeed for the world. It is an encouragement to make peace with each other, to look out for and look after the very needy. The root of Jesse – the beginnings of Jesus – is a signal for us as to how life could be. Pre-Christmas frenzy has been around for a while now; pre-Christmas calm and conversion is the gift of Advent. In Psalm 71 the prayer is for peace and justice, which are two of the deepest longings of humanity.

Reading

Matthew 15: 29–37

After Jesus had left that place, he passed along the Sea of Galilee, and he went up the mountain, where he sat down. Great crowds came to him, bringing with them the lame, the maimed, the blind, the mute, and many others. They put them at his feet, and he cured them, so that the crowd was amazed when they saw the mute speaking, the maimed whole, the lame walking, and the blind seeing. And they praised the God of Israel.

Then Jesus called his disciples to him and said, 'I have compassion for the crowd, because they have been with me now for three days and have nothing to eat; and I do not want to send them away hungry, for they might faint on the way.' The disciples said to him, 'Where are we to get enough bread in the desert to feed so great a crowd?' Jesus asked them, 'How many loaves have you?' They said, 'Seven, and a few small fish.' Then ordering the crowd to sit down on the ground, he took the seven loaves and the fish; and after giving thanks he broke them and gave them to the disciples, and the disciples gave them to the crowds. And all of them ate and were filled; and they took up the broken pieces left over, seven baskets full.

Reflect

This gospel goes further with another meal and gives us a clue of what salvation might mean. The people who had come to Jesus really needed help, healing and forgiveness, and all that goes to make up salvation. They were in bad health; the shores of the sea of Galilee were quickly becoming the A&E of the area. They were very hungry, as we would be if we were waiting for treatment for a long time. Jesus offered salvation with his cures and with his supply of bread and fish for the meal. Salvation is not just for the next life but for all the ways we need wholeness in our lives now. Advent is waiting in hope in the darkness of life, be it spiritual, emotional or physical.

Talk to God

- Lord Jesus, Master of both the light and the darkness, send your Holy Spirit upon our preparations for Christmas. We who have so much to do seek quiet spaces to hear your voice each day, we who are anxious over many things look forward to your coming among us.
- All-powerful God, increase our strength of will for doing good that Christ may find an eager welcome at his coming and call us to his side in the kingdom of heaven, where he lives and reigns with you and the Holy Spirit, one God, for ever and ever. Amen.
- We thank you, Lord, for coming among us, and beginning life as all of us did, in our mother's womb.

SESSION 2

Invitation to Stillness

As you come into God's presence, know that God is already here, waiting for you. Allow yourself to let go of any tensions you may be carrying in your body, allowing the muscles to relax from your head, neck and face, all down your spine and lower body to your feet. Let the stillness take over and lead you to a space where you can make room for the God of dreams to be with you.

Reading

Isaiah 30:19–21.23–24

Truly, O people in Zion, inhabitants of Jerusalem, you shall weep no more. He will surely be gracious to you at the sound of your cry; when he hears it, he will answer you. Though the Lord may give you the bread of adversity and the water of affliction, yet your Teacher will not hide himself any more, but your eyes shall see your Teacher. And when you turn to the right or when you turn to the left, your ears shall hear a word behind you, saying, 'This is the way; walk in it.'

He will give rain for the seed with which you sow the ground, and grain, the produce of the ground, which will be rich and plenteous. On that day your cattle will graze in broad pastures; and the oxen and donkeys that till the ground will eat silage, which has been winnowed with shovel and fork.

Reflect

There are times when we need to hear that 'things will get better'. People say it to us, and often it rings true. Isaiah's reading today is that things will get better for God's people – they will get home. He uses all sorts of imagery: rain for the fields, nourishing bread, animals with plenty to eat, flowing streams in the wilderness and bright lights to kill the darkness. The Lord is the Lord of consolation, inviting us to faith in the promises of God's word. In preparing for Advent we can look forward to the best of life: friendship, gifts and thoughtfulness in family life and in our relationships, and the promise of God's help and support in all of our lives.

Reading

Luke 5:17–26

One day, while he was teaching, Pharisees and teachers of the law were sitting nearby (they had come from every village of Galilee and Judea and from Jerusalem); and the power of the Lord was with him to heal. Just then some men came, carrying a paralysed man on a bed. They were trying to bring him in and lay him before Jesus; but finding no way to bring him in because of the crowd, they went up on the roof and let him down with his bed through the tiles into the middle of the crowd in front of Jesus. When he saw their faith, he said, 'Friend, your sins are forgiven you.' Then the scribes and the Pharisees began to question, 'Who is this who is speaking blasphemies? Who can forgive sins but God alone?' When Jesus perceived their questionings, he answered them, 'Why do you raise such questions in your hearts? Which is easier, to say, "Your sins are forgiven you", or to say, "Stand up and walk"? But so that you may know that the Son of Man has authority on earth to forgive sins' – he said to the one who was paralysed – 'I say to you, stand up and take your bed and go to your home.' Immediately he stood up before them, took what he had been lying on, and went to his home, glorifying God. Amazement seized all of them, and they glorified God and were filled with awe, saying, 'We have seen strange things today.'

Reflect

They saw strange things, the people who were there for the visit of Jesus. They saw a roof being stripped and a stretcher let down in front of Jesus. They saw a row with religious leaders. They heard that sins were forgiven, and they saw a disabled man walk again. He was amazed, too, and the stretcher he brought home would be a souvenir for ever of the best day of his life – the day he met Jesus. Jesus always has something to offer. Any time we pray, we are the better for it. In meeting him there is healing of the soul, of griefs and hurts and the forgiveness of sins. Christmas and our preparation for it is a time of peace, joy, hope and of the total forgiveness of God.

Talk to God

- God of power and mercy, open our hearts in welcome. Remove the things that hinder us from receiving Christ with joy so that we may share his wisdom and become one with him when he comes in glory, for he lives and reigns with you and the Holy Spirit, one God, for ever and ever.
- Thank you, Lord, for forgiveness of sin and for healing of the effects of sin. Let your grace strengthen us in living our Christian life.
- Give peace, O Lord, to family, friends and all your people; peace of mind and heart, and peace to the world.

SESSION 3

Invitation to Stillness

Begin this time of prayer and reflection by paying attention to your breathing, without changing the rhythm. Notice your breathing in and your breathing out – the rhythm, the depth, the feel of the air entering and leaving your mouth or nose.

Reading

Isaiah 35:1–10

      The wilderness and the dry land shall be glad,
         the desert shall rejoice and blossom;
      like the crocus it shall blossom abundantly,

and rejoice with joy and singing.
The glory of Lebanon shall be given to it,
    the majesty of Carmel and Sharon.
They shall see the glory of the LORD,
    the majesty of our God.

Strengthen the weak hands,
    and make firm the feeble knees.
Say to those who are of a fearful heart,
    'Be strong, do not fear!
Here is your God.
    He will come with vengeance,
with terrible recompense.
    He will come and save you.'

Then the eyes of the blind shall be opened,
    and the ears of the deaf unstopped;
then the lame shall leap like a deer,
    and the tongue of the speechless sing for joy.
For waters shall break forth in the wilderness,
    and streams in the desert;
the burning sand shall become a pool,
    and the thirsty ground springs of water;
the haunt of jackals shall become a swamp.

Reflect

We all know people who cause things to happen
by simply being around us: good humour, good

conversation, generosity. They might be people we remember from childhood even. It was a good night when they came to the house. The same is true of today's prophecy from Isaiah. Our God is coming, and things will happen. Blind people will see, deaf people hear, creation will be filled with springs of water and the paths will be safe. What do we expect for Advent? If God is really to come among us soon, we can expect to be filled with amazement. It's not enough to admire the baby of Bethlehem, we have to be amazed that this baby is God-among-us, Emmanuel. The rest of the Gospel will spell out what we are amazed at – the things that Isaiah said would happen when God is with us.

Reading

Matthew 21:23–27

When he entered the temple, the chief priests and the elders of the people came to him as he was teaching, and said, 'By what authority are you doing these things, and who gave you this authority?' Jesus said to them, 'I will also ask you one question; if you tell me the answer, then I will also tell you by what authority I do these things. Did the baptism of John come from heaven, or was it of human origin?' And they argued with one another, 'If we say, "From heaven", he will say to us, "Why then did you not believe him?" But if we say, "Of human origin", we are afraid of the crowd; for all regard John as a prophet.' So they answered Jesus, 'We do not know.' And he said to them, 'Neither will I tell you by what authority I am doing these things.'

Reflect

John is a big figure of Advent, the one who called his people to change their way of life so as to be able to receive the Messiah. John knew that his baptism came from God and that many would refuse it. This would be the same for Jesus in his life: as John's Gospel said later, 'He came among his own people and his own people did not welcome him.' We make sure that in all the celebrations before Christmas – secular and religious – we remember the one who is to come. He will come at Christmas, and he will come all during the year.

Talk to God

- Lord God, may we, your people, who look forward to the birthday of Christ experience the joy of salvation and celebrate that feast with love and thanksgiving. We ask this through Christ our Lord.
- Come, Lord Jesus, into this world of yours, which needs your presence and love.
- Give joy and good health, O Lord, to all we meet this day.

SESSION 4

Invitation to Stillness

Come to this time of quiet prayer with a desire to be still and present to God. Perhaps your mind is racing, perhaps this feels like wasted time, when life is so busy. You can offer God the gift of this time and allow the minutes to flow by, without measuring or counting. Breathing in and out, allow yourself to rest in the moment.

Reading

Genesis 49:2.8–10

Assemble and hear, O sons of Jacob;
   listen to Israel your father.

'Judah, your brothers shall praise you;
   your hand shall be on the neck of your
      enemies;
   your father's sons shall bow down before you.
Judah is a lion's whelp;
   from the prey, my son, you have gone up.
He crouches down, he stretches out like a lion,
   like a lioness – who dares rouse him up?
The sceptre shall not depart from Judah,
   nor the ruler's staff from between his feet,
until tribute comes to him;
   and the obedience of the peoples is his.'

Reflect

How we like to go back over the family! The author reflects on Jacob's words written large in the family history. Future generations would often remember Jacob's words, even though he was signalling out the one for leadership, the favourite son. God's people often went back to the ways God cared for them, and how he used different types of leader. The word and meaning of God's revelation has always been dependent on the men and women of the time. Reflect today on the people in your family who have shared their faith with you; think of them as you prepare for Christmas.

Reading

John 5:33–36

'You sent messengers to John, and he testified to the truth. Not that I accept such human testimony, but I say these things so that you may be saved. He was a burning and shining lamp, and you were willing to rejoice for a while in his light. But I have a testimony greater than John's. The works that the Father has given me to complete, the very works that I am doing, testify on my behalf that the Father has sent me.'

Reflect

We're still being reminded of John the Baptist as Jesus refers to him and his message of truth. The preaching of John was a lamp alight but nothing compared to the light of Jesus. Jesus often refers to light in the Gospel of John. We are to live in the light so that our goodness can be seen, and he describes himself as the 'light of the world'. We live our lives under various lights. Like a bulb in a room, some are brighter than others. Jesus enlightens our whole human life: our sorrows and joys, our loves and apathies, our hopes and dreams. His words enlighten our lives because he is sent by the Father. As we think of the child coming at Advent, we can think of the light of heaven reaching earth.

Talk to God

- Open our minds to receive the Spirit who prepares us for his coming.
- Open our hearts to welcome the Christ child with love and joy.
- Increase our faith in God among us, Emmanuel. We ask this through Christ our Lord.

Prayer for Advent

Loving Father,
Help us remember the birth of Jesus,
that we may share in the song of the angels,
the gladness of the shepherds,
and worship of the wise men.

Close the door of hate
and open the door of love all over the world.
Let kindness come with every gift
and good desires with every greeting.
Deliver us from evil by the blessing
which Christ brings,
and teach us to be merry with clear hearts.

May the Christmas morning
make us happy to be thy children,
and Christmas evening bring us to our beds
with grateful thoughts,
forgiving and forgiven,
for Jesus' sake.
Amen.